Godot Arrives

Books by Nathaniel Hutner

Heracleitus Under Water 1988

War: A Book Of Poems 2003

The Name We Never Lose 2019

The Complete Poems of Nathaniel Hutner 2021

❦

Plays by Nathaniel Hutner

Godot Arrives

Godot Imagine Godot

Godot at Night

Godot, Alive or Dead

The President Pardons Godot

❦

Short Plays by Nathaniel Hutner

Hot Potatoes

The Fix

Keewaydin Plays

Godot Arrives

ෆා

A Comedy by Nathaniel Hutner

Burlington, Vermont

A collected edition of Nathaniel Hutner's plays, *The Collected Plays of Nathaniel Hutner*, is available from Onion River Press, 191 Bank Street, Burlington, VT 05401

Copyright © 2021 by Nathaniel Hutner

All rights reserved. No part of this publication may be reproduced, distributed, or transmitted in any form or by any means, including photocopying, recording, or other electronic or mechanical methods, without the prior written permission of the publisher, except in the case of brief quotations embodied in critical reviews and certain other noncommercial uses permitted by copyright law.

Onion River Press
191 Bank Street
Burlington, VT 05401

ISBN: 978-1-949066-88-3

Library of Congress Control Number: 2021913784

Designed by Jenny Lyons, Middlebury VT

Godot Arrives

CAST OF CHARACTERS

GODOT

DANIEL: Adopted son of A & B

A & B: Two forgotten Apostles

MISS PRIMP: Royal Court Tennis Enthusiast

MISS LUST: Sex Specialist

PROFESSOR FISH: Putative Academic

TOFF I: Snob

TOFF II: Explorer

DR. GODOT: Psychiatrist, distant relative of Godot

MR. TOPS: Clinical Psychologist, Miss Lust's Assistant

POZZO & LUCKY: Representatives of the Old Order

ACT I

A

An abandoned baby!

B

Does it talk?
(Baby makes noise)

A

Evidently.

B

A foreign language. Perhaps it will be good company.

A

Other people's babies usually are.

B

Are you sure it's not ours?

A

Not very likely, though I do admit I'm fond of you.

B

I think it wants to be fed.

A

A rutabaga?

>B

And two carrots?

>A

Perhaps it has a strong digestion.

>B

I don't think we even have water.

>A

I am forecasting rain.

>B

Yes, it will probably arrive with Godot.

>A

It always seems to.

>B

Now we are three.

>A

So there's hope.

>B

Yes, and a future.

>A

Perhaps we should take care of our future.

>B

When we were a couple, it didn't really much matter. It was mostly erections and suicide. And time.

>A

I'm not fond of time.

>B

It seems to be infinite, wherever you look.

>A

Appalling.

B
Do you suppose it's infinite in the afterlife?

A
I don't see how anyone could stand it, even in the afterlife.

B
I would choose to be eternally present.

A
Stop with paradoxes.

B
But the baby.

A
We haven't diapers.

B
Just leave the pants off — it will pee al fresco.

A
I wonder how it feels, being abandoned.

B
Is it a he or a she?

A
He.

B
We may get in trouble with the Authorities.

A
Wait till Godot arrives.

B
He will arrange things.

A
He already has.

      B
Perhaps Godot's in the afterlife by now.

      A
He may be, in which case, we've got heavy-duty trucking ahead. I think a prayer might help. Let me see … "May the grace that gives life beauty, and the love that hallows it, be with us all."

      B
Ooohh.
(Baby gurgles appreciatively)

      A
Would you care for a hymn?

      B
Not likely.

      A
A moment of meditation?

      B
I'm anti-clerical.

      A
A mantra's just what you want.

      B
Vamoose.

(A goes offstage. B approaches child, coos over it and allows a finger to be clasped in its fist. Baby smiles. B smiles back; both baby and B are pleased. A comes back onstage and watches the other two before speaking)

      A
Well, that's encouraging.

      B
I know, I can't help it.

    A
Paternal piety — fidus Achates.

    B
We'll have to apply for custody.

    A
I think we've already been elected by default.

    B
Well.

    A
Not that I object.

    B
It would have been better if we had been sounded out. Then again, when has that ever happened? And now this one arrives, without even a dog-tag. Well, there's no one else here, so it's us or utter abandonment.

    A
Don't you find him appealing?

    B
Of course, only now we have to assume one more burden, another anxiety.

    A
Think of the joy he will bring.

    B
I can't wait.

    A
And when he's grown —

    B
When he's grown he'll write a nasty book about us and publish it in twelve languages.

> A

Cynic.

> B

I am a highly pragmatic person.

> A

What of the transforming power of love?

> B

You ask me that?

> A

Sorry.

> B

And what do we do when Godot arrives? How do we explain the excess baggage?

> A

Not to worry. It's for him to explain.

> B

I suppose. Do you know how to coo?

> A

I'm a little out of practice. I think I gave it up around age one. Before I start that, what should we call the little one?

> B

Hope? Faith? Charity?

> A

It's not female.

> B

How about something biblical? Or Greek?

> A

Daniel. Who slew the lion —

B
Yes. Yes …

A
It's appropriate, if you consider what we've got ahead of us.

B
One vast opportunity.

A
One big mess.

B
Call in the mops.

A
Call in — Daniel.

B
We'll never see him once he's grown.

A
If we live that long.

B
It's a good name.

A
Better than Pozzo.

B
Better than Lucky.

A
Where are those two, anyway?

B
Whipping their destiny along like a whore.

A
Now we have something better than destiny. We have hope.

B
He's in practice.

A
I've read about this somewhere…

B
Oscar Wilde?

A
The cloak room at Victoria Station!

B
Miss Prism!

A
Shall we call him Earnest?

B
Of course. It's highly appropriate, especially if we are to be the parents.

A
With or without the A?

B
With — after all, that's the point of it.

A
Our own Earnest!

B
Do we burp him now?

A
Yes. You go first.
(Baby burps after a few bounces on B's shoulder)

B
I think he got up more than just air.

    A
I'll clean you. There.

    B
Now for a nap, Daniel Earnest.

    A
Quite adorable. Think. Now we have someone to live for besides ourselves!

    B
Very gratifying.

    A
Not that I was tiring of you. Still, after the passage of some time, a change in the human landscape can be welcome.

    B
I quite agree.

    A
Oh.

    B
Listen to him laugh.

    A
I was a smiling baby.

    B
What happened?

    A
Those who were insecure thought I was laughing at them and fell away. All but you.

    B
I understood.

    A
Yes.

      B
There he goes again. It's positively heartening.

      A
More useful than a scowl.

      B
It makes for good company.

      A
And optimism as to future developments.

      B
Why do you laugh?

      A
I'm inspired. Who's here?

      MISS PRIMP
Miss Primp. Can you tell me the way to the court?

      B
Royal or sporting?

      A
Why both, of course.

(B ?)

      MISS PRIMP
The Royal Tennis Court. There are only fifteen in the world, and I have played on them all.

      A
Did you win your match?

      MISS PRIMP
That is not what matters. I play to bolster my opinion of myself. Royal tennis props me up. It's a tonic.

      A
Oh.

MISS PRIMP
Yes. And the exercise is vigorous. I adore vigor.

A
That's not the only thing you adore.

MISS PRIMP
Quite right. I also adore Mr. Godot.

A
Have you seen him?

MISS PRIMP
Not quite. But I have heard volumes. Volumes. The philosophers would say I know him by acquaintance — by hearsay. I do. I know him intimately by hearsay. And there is very much to know.

B
We expect him.

MISS PRIMP
Mr. Godot?

B
Yes. Presently.

MISS PRIMP
How unfortunate. I have a game scheduled for three o'clock which I cannot miss. Do give him my sincere regrets.

B
Yes. We shall.

MISS PRIMP
Well, then, good-bye.

B
Goodbye.

A
Goodbye.

B
I wonder if she knows how to read a ouija board?

A
Not likely.

B
Have you ever wished to know your future?

A
Not likely.

B
Would sort of deflate everything, eh? Destroy your sense of freedom, make you a victim of determinism?

A
What?

B
Well, everything would happen according to plan. You would choose what you knew you would choose, and so on. There would be no room for the unexpected.

A
I ask myself — how would Godot feel about this?

B
Not very happy, I am sure.

A
Everything foreordained — even for him.

B
Appalling.

A
Well, that is not the case with us. Not yet.

>B

No. We must try to preserve our ignorance. Have you ever heard of Miss Lust?

>A

Who?

>B

Miss Lust. We have an appointment with her today.

>A

Oh, the one that produces vibrations.

>B

Yes.

>A

Well, good heavens, there she is!

>MISS LUST

I am Miss Lust.

>A

You know Godot?

>MISS LUST

Yes, we are intimately acquainted

>B

You?

>MISS LUST

Certainly. Well, I should say we have been intimately connected in parts.

>A

Good heavens.

>MISS LUST

Precisely. He's very knowledgeable and is always willing to learn. I have taught him many things.

    B
Many things?

    MISS LUST
Of course. No one knows all that I know about, well, lust. Unless I instruct them. Mr. Godot, in fact, was a very apt pupil. He enjoyed learning.

    A
Very apt?

    MISS LUST
Yes.

    B
Well, this is news.

    MISS LUST
I could give you details, but that would be kiss and tell. Ask him when you see him. He is not ashamed to talk of me, of us. He is very kind.

    B
And where are you off to?

    MISS LUST
To play tennis.

    A
Royal tennis?

    MISS LUST
Yes.

    A
I think you have a partner just ahead of you.

    MISS LUST
Either gender will do.
(A and B: raised eyebrows)

A
I wonder if there is a Mr. Lust.

B
You tell me.
(A and B exchange glances)

A
Do you suppose?

B
But it was so long ago.

A
Do you still feel that way, even a little?

B
Sometimes. I have really never been able to get over you.

A
How handsome we were.

B
Yes.

A
How much in love.

B
Yes.

A
We thought — well, we never thought of us, here.

B
No. But we lived.

A
And still do, to a degree.

B
Look: Daniel's smiling.

A
It will be much different for him than for us.

B
Externally. Inside, I think the feelings are the same whatever way you turn out.

A
Another visitor!

B
What is this place, Piccadilly Circus?

PROFESSOR FISH
I am Professor Fish.

A
A man of parts!

PROFESSOR FISH
Yes. A Bachelor of Parts, a Master of Ceremonies, and Doctor of Verbal Disturbances.

B
Quite a combination.

PROFESSOR FISH
I am versatile.

B
Have you any idea why we are here?

PROFESSOR FISH
No.

B
To pass the time.

A
You seem to have passed your time quite well.

PROFESSOR FISH
I would really like to be an actor.

B
Why the degrees?

PROFESSOR FISH
I did so well in kindergarten, I just kept going.

A
Acting's not for everyone.

B
Don't be so sure.

PROFESSOR FISH
I lecture poorly, my students detest me in tutorial, and my research is renowned throughout the world. Not that anybody will be reading it fifty years from now.

A
In the meantime, your students abandon the fields you teach because you turn them off.

PROFESSOR FISH
I hadn't thought of that.

B
Professors rarely do.

A
If you ask me, it's all a racket anyway — like most professions. The pupils' parents pay the fees, the pupils drink beer and learn how to fornicate, and after four years they collect their diplomas and go out into the world, where they cash them in and fornicate some more.

PROFESSOR FISH
Cash them in?

A
Yes. They cash in their diplomas for the rest of their lives, particularly if the diploma is from a highly-rated institution. A diploma bordered in crimson gives you a lot of mileage, not only at work, but also in casual conversation at cocktail parties.

B
I never speak about mine.

A
I know. You don't believe in labels.

PROFESSOR FISH
Oh!

B
It's true. With all your degrees, you're just another professor to me, covered with labels.

A
And there are plenty of professors about, even bordered with crimson.

PROFESSOR FISH
Oh!

B
Don't worry, the rest of us don't know the important questions — or answers — any better than you do. You just pretend to. The fact is, you're a professor because you can bear to read three books a week — and even that pace you don't keep up past age thirty. Well, I can read, too, but I would much rather spend my time outside, with our tree, our baby —

A
And me.

B
And Miss Primp and Miss Lust and — surprise — you.

PROFESSOR FISH
I manipulate words, not people.

B
It can come to the same thing. Look at me, a poet manqué, who can turn most situations to account, often without knowing it.

PROFESSOR FISH
Peculiar.

B
Not really. All you have to do is stick around and keep your eyes open. Then you either practice or you're practiced upon.

PROFESSOR FISH
I seem to be the latter.

B
Touché.

A
He really isn't as cynical as he makes out. He just wishes he was innocent again, and since he's not, he gets angry and indulges himself by pretending he's wicked. It's a common psychological game. All wind, below decks.

B
You're too true.

A
You will be, too, if you want.

B
(To PROFESSOR FISH)
It is very likely that you would know more if you knew less.

A
Drop the books.

                B
Take up bar-hopping.

                A
Bridge.

                B
Baseball.

                A
Acting.

                PROFESSOR FISH
Ah!

                B
Learn to improvise.

                A
Tell dirty stories.

                B
Collect bottle caps.

                A
You see?

                PROFESSOR FISH
When do I start?

                B
Right now. There is a Royal Tennis Court just off there to the left. You will like it.

                PROFESSOR FISH
Thank you so much, both of you! I really didn't care for Plotinus anyway.

                A
Not at all.

    B
Not at all.

    A
Just remember James Joyce.

    PROFESSOR FISH
How so?

    A
He thought he would fool the Professors, but the Professors fooled him.

    PROFESSOR FISH
How do you mean?

    A
Who reads Finnegans Wake?

    PROFESSOR FISH
Yes.

    B
Off with you!

    A
How's the little one?

    B
Taking a snooze.

    A
Ahhh!

    B
Not you. You're not a professor yet. And he wanted to be an actor.

    A
He was.

    B
Your wit is irremediable.

    A
You are too.

    B
Do you know what time it is?

    A
I would say twoish. Of course, it's hard to say precisely: the sun has got unreliable in the modern era, what with Relativity, and the Waste Land. We are all adrift in an empty room, and so on.

    B
I wouldn't have minded being Caesar. All that solid accomplishment.

    A
I think the Christians ruined everything: their ideal is self-abnegation. If you have any scruples at all, success ceases to be sweet.

    B
Well, here we are.

    A
But we're not Christian.

    B
We must have been at one point, or we wouldn't be here.

    A
And consider chastity.

    B
I never did, even when I was alone.

    A
More's the point. It just is not human nature to be chaste;

and those who are generally have no choice. They pretend to despise what they secretly crave.

    B

A few have no cravings, and for them there is nothing to give up.

    A

Like turtle soup.

    B

For Lent.

    A

How about the Confessional?

    B

Talk about rackets. The Church makes a thousand impossible demands on you. Surprise — you fall into sin. So then you feel guilty and voilà, see the Father Confessor, who makes you whole again. Then back to square one.

    A

Sounds like emotional blackmail.

    B

Bingo!

    A

Is there another way?

    B

You had best consult your imagination.

    A

But —

    B

I know it's work, but try.

  A
But I can't answer any of the important questions.
  B
That's a beginning.
  A
I proceed from there?
  B
Correct.
  A
And create my life as I go along —
  B
Like an artist of the soul.
  A
I shall try to grow.
  B
Even to the end.
  A
Look!
  B
One more weary voyager.
  TOFF I
Halloo!
  B
A prototypical toff.
  A
Of what is he the fruition?
  B
We shall see.

TOFF I
Is either of you a Jew?

B
If not by birth, then certainly in spirit.

TOFF I
I am a pillar of society, I reside in a very exclusive neighborhood, I own a Rolls, I know Politicians to whom I make generous gifts, I am a vestryman of my church, I speak French and adore the Opera, I sit on fashionable Boards, my children play with the sons and daughters of famous publishers, artists, investment bankers, lawyers, clergy; I even play polo when invited and can shoot pheasant; I have a country-house, a wife that rides a horse, my reputation is of the highest order — and I went to Harvard.

B
Call no man happy until he is safe in the grave.

TOFF I
I am very far from it.

B
You live perpetually at its edge —

A
Death is a very good guide in life.

B
It keeps you on your toes.

TOFF I
How morbid.

B
I guarantee it.

A
It is inevitable.

B
And if you don't learn it here, there is plenty of space elsewhere for you to learn it in.

A
You will only be finding yourself.

TOFF I
Nonsense. I have told you who I am.
(A and B exhange glances)

TOFF I
(Continued)
I am Mr. Toff, and I command respect from all who know me. Perhaps I require more from life than others. That is my privilege.

B
Well said.

A
But watch out for that edge.

TOFF I
Nonsense. I must go. I am late for a luncheon appointment.

A
Goodbye.

B
Goodbye.

TOFF I
Good riddance.

A
Do I see his twin approaching?

B
I believe so.

A
Same clothes, same tilt, same complexion.

B
The nose is smaller.

A
Not aquiline.

B
My grandfather had an aquiline nose — he was very distinguished. He believed in co-operatives.

TOFF II
Hello. A bit gusty.

A
Yes.

TOFF II
You're not cold?

A
Well, yes, somewhat.

TOFF II
Here, it fits you better than it did me.

A
Oh!

B
Good heavens, a manneqin.

A
No. Just a man.

TOFF II
I am Sir William Toff II.

B
I am B.

    A
I am A.

    TOFF II
I have been to Ethiopia, the Sudan, the Outer Hebrides, and so on. But I always come home.

    A
You must tell us what the world is like, at least the parts we don't already know.

    TOFF II
Well, curiously enough, the people are much the same. It is their circumstances that change.

    A
But that is true even if you stay at home.

    TOFF II
Indeed.

    A
Then why did you go?

    TOFF II
Like the Roman soldier in Lucretius, I was trying to get away from myself.

    B
You'll manage soon enough — none of us is immortal.

    A
Yes. We just wait and watch.

    TOFF II
I like activity.

    B
But not action.

A
I meant to ask: did you ever find yourself?

TOFF II
With you, here, I feel for the first time that I may look inside and not be appalled.

A
Oh, we've been appalled.

B
It wears off after a bit.

A
You find out soon enough that, as you said, everyone's pretty much the same.

B
You just have more scruples than usual. That is all.

TOFF II
I shall need a new occupation.

A
How do you stand financially?

TOFF II
Dead broke.

B
A person of your station?

TOFF II
Travel is not the best way to make money, and I am a younger son of a younger son. My father was an Egyptian civil servant.

A
Do you have any unique talents?

TOFF II
I can smell out the truth about people.

  B
Hurrah.

  TOFF II
That's the advantage of traveling. You see everything.

  B
And —

  A
Shh.

  TOFF II
And I can turn a phrase.

  A
A poet!

  B
He has no occupation, he has no money, he's perspicuous about people and he can turn a phrase. A natural. Have you ever written verse?

  TOFF II
Well…

  A
You needn't be shy with us.

  TOFF II
If you like, I'll recite one of my better (!) efforts. Ready? It's a Comment on War:

> Now Reason's drowned
> Amidst a flood of fools fearing fools,
> And Folly's crowned
> With witless words, our witless minds to rule.

  A
Bravo.

    B
Very good for an initiate. Could we anoint you Poet Laureate?
Everyone should have a title; titles grease the wheels of Society.

    TOFF II
But I haven't any money.

    B
Most of Society doesn't either, until they get married.

    TOFF II
I have no desire to get married.

    A
That's all right, we love you already.

    B
You really are a poet.

    TOFF II
Of life, and now of words.

    B
More than words.

    A
We people may be similar in as many ways as you have seen, but few of us claim poetry as our purpose in life.

    TOFF II
I have very little to lose.

    B
And we have much to gain.

    A
Remember, in this field volume does not count: one poem, truly written, admits you to the fellowship of the word.

    B
And you can never be tossed out.

      A
As for your personal life —
(B coughs)

      TOFF II
Meeting you two is quite an experience.

      A
And we're not even in the Outer Hebrides.

      B
We're close.

      A
Do you have another poem?

      TOFF II
Well, my repertoire is limited, but I think I can do one more:

> Blue leaf leave me,
> Blue metal on the lawn,
> The long way down
> Is new to me
> Though not new to all.
> White fire of dew
> On leaves, white steel
> Of dew, turn to ice
> On fallen trees,
> Turn to ice in fall.

      A
Definitely Poet Laureate material. We, the Committee of Two, nominate you. Any opposed? You are elected.

      TOFF II
That's new.

      A
We do what we can.

> B
>
> Much more.

> TOFF II
>
> You make me weep.

> A
>
> A toff — and you weep?

> TOFF II
>
> I walk into the desert and find friends, a home and an occupation, as well as myself.

> A
>
> Would you care for a rutabaga?

> B
>
> Carrots?

> A
>
> And we'll have water as soon as it rains.

> B
>
> Yes.

> TOFF II
>
> I have seen men die, but I have never seen them so true.

> A
>
> Well, now you have.

> B
>
> Try to repeat the experience.

> A
>
> We've forgotten Daniel!

> B
>
> He was sleeping.

> A
>
> Would you care to meet — our child?

TOFF II
Is this an example of Parthenogenesis?

A
I don't know. But we have adopted an orphan.

B
Yes, even though our union has never been solemnized, Fate has made us parents. You're beaming.

A
Yes. It is a great pleasure to be loved by the young. It was something I didn't expect.

TOFF II
Most true gifts are.

B
(To TOFF II)
I can learn from you.

A
(To B)
You already are.

TOFF II
May I hold him — is it Daniel?

A
Oh, yes.

B
And his middle name is Earnest.

A
With an "A".

B
It's our personal plaisanterie.

TOFF II
Daniel. Well.

A
If you look deeply into your own child, you will find a good part of yourself.

TOFF II
Ohhh.

A
How's Daniel?

TOFF II
Bubbly. He looks like both his Daddies. It's odd: an orphan.

A
And we've had apples, too.

B
And many visitors. Even here.

A
Near the Outer Hebrides.

B
On the heath.
We weep, like you. We've always liked company. And we don't talk politics. — But that's something else.

TOFF II
Well, here is Daniel. I must go on.

A
If you care for Royal Tennis, just turn left over there. You'll find some people playing already. I'm told it's quite an exclusive game. As Poet Laureate you'll fit right in. You can be a spectator. Action should always have a home in reflection.

       B
And vice versa.

       A
Goodbye.

       B
Goodbye.

     TOFF II
Ciao.

       A
Would anyone care to take a photograph?

       B
I could send one to my mother.

       A
Where is she?

       B
Waiting for Godot, last I heard.

       A
Even photographs lie.

       B
Pretty depressing.

       A
How's Daniel?

       B
O.K.

       A
I wonder when he'll begin?

       B
To lie?

    A
Uh-huh.

    B
Perhaps we should put him in training.

    A
I'm not aware that we ever lied.

    B
We spared ourselves — for this...
(Looks around)

    A
I hope Daniel takes after us in that.

    B
Good heavens!

    A
What?

    B
Look! Another apple!

    A
It seems we inhabit the Garden of Eden.

    B
We could sell cider. Ouch.

    A
I shall make a pie for Daniel. I shall use Mrs. Cray's recipe.

    B
Mrs. Cray?

    A
My nursemaid. Before we met.

    B
I'm glad to hear it, happy to have company.

A
Do you suppose it's Mackintosh?

B
Northern Spy?

A
Red Empire?

B
Delicious?

A
That's odd. There seem to be different varieties — from the same tree.

B
There you have it.

A
Plucked from the mud.

DR. GODOT
I am Dr. Godot, Analyst-in-Chief of the Magdalene Mental Mercyseat.

B
Sounds grand.

A
Any relation —

DR. GODOT
Of course. We are fourth cousins twelve times removed.

B
Ah, a voice in the choir. I believe we know each other.

DR. GODOT
(Examining him carefully)
Yes, you may have been a patient. I am an authority on

masochism. I remember that you had a curious compulsion — which we won't discuss — as well as paranoid tendencies.

      B

The world being what it is…

      DR. GODOT

Yes, you suffered enormously.

      A

I am glad to hear it.

(B and DR. GODOT look at A)

      A

(Continued)

It makes us that much closer, one to the other. It is something we have in common, besides love.

      DR. GODOT

Yes, pain is a paradox. And logicians know that a paradox implies any proposition.

      A

Proposition? Let's not be vulgar.

      B

Darling.

      DR. GODOT

I have come to administer a follow-up examination on you.

      B

Thirty years later?

      DR. GODOT

There were some minor funding problems.

      B

You mean it took you thirty years to pay off the Department of Mental Health?

> DR. GODOT
>
> That and the paperwork. And what with committee meetings, grant applications and so forth, I have only now found the time to pursue one of my most illuminating cases.

> B
>
> Well, here I am...

> DR. GODOT
>
> What do you live on?

> B
>
> Water. When it rains.

> DR. GODOT
>
> Any children?

> B
>
> I have adopted an orphan, with A here.

> DR. GODOT
>
> Are you on medication?

> B
>
> Not that I know.

> DR. GODOT
>
> Any loss of memory?

> B
>
> Voluntary or involuntary?

> DR. GODOT
>
> Involuntary.

> B
>
> I remember what bothers me.

> DR. GODOT
>
> I'll put down involuntary. Do you still have any paranoid phantasies?

                B
Only if they have a basis in fact.

>   DR. GODOT
Married?
(B gestures to A)

>   DR. GODOT
(Continued)
Oh. Any plans to alter your marital status?

>   B
I'd rather die first.
(A smiles)

>   DR. GODOT
Any problems with insomnia?

>   B
Only when the moon is full and there are no clouds.

>   DR. GODOT
Please count to ten.
(B does so)

>   DR. GODOT
(Continued)
Now please count backwards from ten.
(B balks)

>   A
He never was a math whiz.

>   DR. GODOT
All right. One more question: are your emotions overwhelming, available but under control, or absent?

>   B
They are available and for the most part I control them. When I am provoked, they control me.

DR. GODOT
Not bad.

B
Is that it?

DR. GODOT
For now. Thank you.
(To A)
Thank you.
(DR. GODOT exits)

A
I guess he's not into tennis.

B
Too many things on his mind. 30 years???

A
Leave it. If he comes back, we can worry ourselves then. And please don't fill me in — your past is not pertinent here. We must tend to the young one.

B
One day he'll have a happy past. It's our gift to him.

A
Yes.

GODOT
Lively time.

A
Who?

B
What was that?

GODOT
I say, you've had a more than usually lively day.

A
Are you planning to contribute?

GODOT
Indeed. If you will allow me.

B
You sure are starched.

GODOT
I'm a bit out of date. There. I usually try to suit my surroundings.

B
Oh. I'm B, this is A.

GODOT
Enchanté.

B
And you.

A
Yes.

GODOT
Call me Max.

A
Nothing else?

GODOT
Not for the moment.

A
Well, it's simple.

B
Max?

GODOT
Yes.

    B
You come from these parts?

    GODOT
Amongst others. Tell me, have you been waiting long?

    A
Since we were born.

    B
Approximately two millennia.

    GODOT
Your patience becomes you.

    B
Indeed.

    GODOT
And — for whom do you wait?

    A
Oh, Godot.

    GODOT
Friend, acquaintance?

    B
Savior. Who are you, the Prince of Perplexity?

    GODOT
And this Godot, who is he?

    A
We're not certain. But we know that —

    B
We know nothing.

    GODOT
Evidently.

A
We would like to know something, as a matter of course.

GODOT
Well, everything is worth something, and some things may be worth everything.

B
Touché.
(Grins)

A
May I quote you?

GODOT
Of course.

A
You are easy, aren't you?

GODOT
I try to please.

B
Good luck.

A
You remind me of Cupid.

GODOT
That has been said of me before.

A
Do you suppose Cupid was allowed a lover of his own?

GODOT
Highly unlikely.

A
Why do you say that?

GODOT
He would have to be partial to one over the rest — for him an impossible situation.

A
And so he goes loveless?

GODOT
I am afraid that is the case.

A
To be fair to everyone, he must love them all equally?

GODOT
Right.

A
It's a neat trick.

GODOT
I've always thought a God, Roman or otherwise, should be allowed at least one personal attachment. But then gods are highly impersonal, especially Modern gods.

A
If I did without B, I would be nowhere.

GODOT
Yes.

A
And Daniel.

GODOT
Is he a God?

A
Not yet.

GODOT
(Pained expression)
And do you know why you wait?

B
We are out of work. Temporarily.

A
In the autumn we pick apples.

GODOT
By then it's too late.

A
Excuse me?

GODOT
I say, how long do people live around here? I mean, what is the normal span of life?

A
It all depends on diet.

B
Rutabaga.

A
Carrots.

GODOT
And you two?

A
It's hard to predict.

B
If you like your occupation, you may go on indefinitely.
(GODOT: pained expression)

A
Of course, retirement is generally required.

B
Then we drop like stones.

A
Boredom.

B
Emptiness

A
Loneliness.

B
Anguish in the face of the unknown.

A
That is not new.

B
No.

A
But we all suffer, one way or another.

GODOT
And who arranged things this way?

A
Well, Mr. Godot is supposed to arrive soon, and I'm sure he'll give you an answer.

GODOT
And Mr. Godot, where does he come from?

A
(Laughs)
That's a good one!

B
He doesn't come, he goes.

GODOT
How will you know him, if he comes?

A
Oh, he's very distinctive. Very noticeable.

B
Yes, we have eyewitness accounts of him that are very reliable.

A
And he has a son, whom some know at first-hand.

GODOT
Any distinctive features for Monsieur Godot?

A
Well, he speaks daggers and his eyes are like fire. He is usually dressed in red and carries a scale in which to weigh souls.

GODOT
Souls?

A
Oh, yes, he is a master of souls; some he sends to Heaven, and the rest go to Hell.

GODOT
Forever?

B
Yes. Forever.

GODOT
I don't think I care much for this Godot. And what is Hell?

A
I'm not quite sure, but I do know you can never get out of it.

GODOT
(Pained expression)
For all eternity?

      B
Indeed.

      GODOT
Well, that much I knew. And so you are waiting.

      B
Yes. Care to join us?

      GODOT
Not right now, thank you.

      A
You look a little depressed.

      GODOT
Thinking of eternity always fatigues me.

      A
Why? the possibilities are limitless.

      GODOT
Precisely.

(A ?)

      GODOT
I prefer something a bit better defined.

      B
Like mortality.

      GODOT
I've tried that too.

      B
Not your bag?

      GODOT
Well, death was very relaxing, but there was not much to it.

      A
Can't you find a compromise?

GODOT
That is why I am here. I have come to consult you two.

A
Three.

GODOT
Three?

A
Don't forget Daniel.

GODOT
Oh! How handsome he is. And which one of you —

B
Both.

GODOT
(?)
Oh. I didn't realize you could...

A
It's an orphan.

B
It's adopted.

A
But we love him more than ourselves.
(GODOT is somewhat pained)

B
Oh, love is in short supply. I'm sure the Authorities would let you adopt, if you want.

GODOT
I'm afraid that's in the same category as marriage — for me.

A
What are you allowed to do?

GODOT
Pretty much what I want. Right now I have arranged things so that I could consult you about the possibility of a compromise?

B
Compromise?

GODOT
Yes. Between mortality and the infinite. For the deuce of me, I cannot come up with an answer. You two (three) spend what time you have face to face with both.

A
Well, we hope to be granted life eternal, you know, when...

GODOT
And you really find the idea of eternal life attractive?

A
I don't suppose it would be much different than what we have now — except we could look forward to its continuing indefinitely into the future.

(Looks puzzled — A and B look around themselves, at themselves)

GODOT
You see what I mean?

A & B
I think so.

GODOT
Do you think that perhaps Mr. Godot has an answer?

A
Very likely.

B
I am convinced of it.

GODOT
Well, please let me know what he says. I must be off. Do let me know —

    A
Bye.

    B
No orphans for him?

    A
Apparently not. Certainly not one like ours.

    B
How is he?

    A
He's asleep. The soul of innocence. I wish I could sleep as he does. I vaguely remember that I did once. An axe! Shall I wound you?

    B
Not likely.

    A
I shall have to get back into shape. But we have no wood.

    B
What about the tree?

    A
It would improve the view.

    B
But we need apples — for Daniel.

    A
Right you are.

    B
Even in small numbers.

    A
Yes. Well, I shall wave it about. That will make potential aggressors think twice.
    B
You will just aggravate them.
    A
Nonsense. We require —
    B
Look, please get rid of that thing. Otherwise you may amputate your nose. Then you would have to move to L.A.
    A
Why?
    B
That's where the plastic surgeons are — I have a grandfather who has just enjoyed his fifth face-lift.
    A
I wonder if I need one.
    B
There are other things you need far more.
    A
I know I'm vain.
    B
Well, we have no mirrors, so you can't encourage yourself. We don't even have a reflecting pool.
    A
We have Daniel. We can see ourselves in him.
    B
No comment.

A
What put you in a bad mood?

B
I am running out of patience.

A
With whom?

B
Life.

A
Would you like an apple?

B
They give you the trots if you eat too many.

A
Then you need cheese.

B
This is ridiculous. All we do is talk.

A
I enjoy conversation.

B
I want action.

A
Sometimes we act, too.

B
Ach!

A
It beats working.

B
That is utterly false. Not-working, not-doing is the hardest work in the world. Every single person I have ever known who

has tried it either went mad, became an alcoholic or committed suicide. I do not refer to Eastern Yogis — they, at least, can meditate.

    A

We can't leave here, we've got to wait for Godot.

    B

Take a look at Daniel. We can wait for him. Imagine him at eighteen — he will find a girl, go to university — he might even thank us for our pains as parents.

    A

Not likely. Did you ever thank your father?

    B

Certainly not. I told him his mistakes.

    A

What about your mother?

    B

She made no mistakes.

    A

That's a mistake.

    B

Yes.

    A

Let us be loving but fallible.

    B

All right. Can you plan these things ahead?

    A

Probably not.

    B

What if he likes one of us more than the other?

A

That's normal, though most religious people I have known say it isn't Christian.

B

(??)

Are we Christians?

A

Well, Unitarians.

B

What on earth is that?

A

One of the more obscure heresies.

B

God knows I've been a heretic. And I am certainly not a Christian. Nobody I know is, even the Christians. Though if they realized that, and tried to improve —

A

We'd have more company.

B

Money!

A

What?

B

I've found money in my shoe!

A

So that's where the pain came from.

B

I've been limping for twenty years! And all the doctors said it was psychological!

A
They were right.

B
Yes. Well, now that we are rich, I propose we eat something. A chocolate shake. For two.

A
For three.

B
Oh. Damn!

A
Yes — we have to save it for Daniel — his shots, his teeth, his clothes — his education.

B
My education didn't cost me anything, except some pain.

A
Daniel must have a proper upbringing.

B
Yes.

A
B, our tree has no leaves.

B
It has apples.

A
But why no leaves?

B
It is old. Leaves are green, and green is the color of youth. Our tree is not young. What it has to offer now is the fruit of its age. And that is what we have to live on.
   "All that lives must dies,
   Passing through nature to eternity."

A
Oooh — you've got back your memory!

B
A few tidbits.

A
That was wonderful. Who said it?

B
I forget.

A
Well, I shall try to remember it, too. Two heads are better than one.

B
Shakespeare.

A
Don't tease. You always were impressive with your quotes. I remember when you had half the Odyssey down, in Greek. No one knew what you were saying, but the sounds were very melodious. Professor Parry would have been happy.

B
Who?

A
Milman. Milman Parry.

B
I'll let that one pass.

(A shrugs)

B
I wonder if Homer made a buck out of poetry. If he did, he was the last.

      A
You can still write for pleasure.

      B
What else <u>could</u> I write for? You used to call me perspicuous, and I was. Poets are proud to see, even more than to write. Well, look around for a while, and you're headed for lunacy or suicide: the occupational hazards of the poet. In self-defense I tried to close my eyes. What happens? I dream! Which is worse than being awake. So I returned to my verse, eyes open. As you may see, my muse and myself are still collaborating.

      A
I always admired your courage.

      B
Thank you. We have to make choices.
(They look at each other. They are very much in love)

      B
(Continued)
What time is it?

      A
Close to sunset.

      B
Miss Primp!

      MISS PRIMP
Yes.

      B
How was your game?

      MISS PRIMP
Superbly invigorating. I adore vigor. Mens sana in corpore sano: Mind and physique in good trim. You should try it. It quite cleans out the brain. And the participants are always

respectable. As a rule, Royal Court Tennis is an infallible test of social acceptability.

    B

The cream may float on top, but so does the scum.

    A

B!

    MISS PRIMP

You said something?

    A

He's on a diet of water and apples — no energy for exercise.

    MISS PRIMP

How unfortunate. I hope his case is not terminal.

    B

Mortality usually is.

    A

B!

    MISS PRIMP

Oh, has Mr. Godot made an appearance?

    A

Not yet.

    B

We think he may have forgotten the time.

    A

It's very easy to do. Especially in fine weather.

    MISS PRIMP

Well don't let him keep you. You must set a time limit, and if he doesn't show up, proceed without him. Otherwise you will be immobilized indefinitely.

                A
Waiting is not a treat.
                B
But we have hope.
                A
And a future.
                MISS PRIMP
That's nice. Well, goodbye. No doubt we shall meet again.
                B
If the fates are kind.
                A
Yes.
                MISS PRIMP
Yes.
                B
So she goes. I wonder if Miss Lust can be far behind.
                A
Aha!
                MISS LUST
Oh!
(B laughs)
                MISS LUST
How delightful to see you again. You know I like handsome men, and both of you are perfectly adorable — just like my pet schnauzer, Ding-a-ling. In fact, I can tell, you all have many characteristics in common. You're alternately anxious and irritable, especially if dinner is not on time; you like to laugh (Ding-a-ling has a charming little whimper, like this…); and you are all gentle, even when it goes against your mood. As you

know, when the atmosphere is heavy, it is my opportunity to provide some warmth, even heat, to those in need.

    B

How did she ever get such a bad press?

    A

I believe it all began with St. Augustine.

    B

Pray, dear God in Heaven, let me be good, but not yet.

    MISS LUST

Is sex not good?

    B

There are those who would have us think so. But, of course, they haven't met you.

    MISS LUST

Oh!

    B

Next time we see one, we'll give you a ring.

    MISS LUST

A new challenge!

    B

I'm certain you'll do yourself credit.

    MISS LUST

I must be off — I have an appointment with Mr. Godot.

(B !)

    MISS LUST

We won't be long — just some evangelizing on behalf of mortality's bright spots. Then he's yours.

(She goes off)

      B
Life's ironies are sometimes quite precious.

      A
Where would we be without her?

      B
That's obvious.

      A
You and I, what would Mr. Godot say?

      B
We are all children of Providence.

      A
We are all children of God.

      B
We are beginning to sound like the Archbishop of Canterbury.

      A
Quite likely. Two more apples.

      B
It must be getting on toward dinner.

      A
Daniel dines first.

      B
May I?
(B takes DANIEL and administers food)

      A
Time for evacuation. Watch out!

      B
That was a bit close. Of course, I've been hit with worse.

      A
Let's leave that alone.

    B
Righto.

    A
What do you think Godot is like?

    B
More revolutionary than the Apocalypse, more reactionary than Death, perfectly persuasive, eternally present, invariably true, merciful and righteous, semi-comic and unitary.

    A
Well. I could use that resumé.

    B
You wouldn't want it.

    A
But he's whatever he wants to be.

    B
That doesn't make him any other than what he is.

    A
Everybody and everything!

    B
You're highly amusing.

    A
Oh, come on, can't you let him alone?

    B
What's the point? He's the only one like him there is, or can be.

    A
He needs a girl.

    B
My foot.

A
He's lonely.

B
Very good.

A
Only he can keep himself company. Only he can be his equal.

B
Ugh.

A
Miss Lust! You're back!

MISS LUST
I always come back. Several times, at the least, even in one day.

B
More news of Godot?

MISS LUST
I hear he has been jettisoning a good part of his powers. He wishes to be like us. A trial run. Omniscience and omnipotence have their deficiencies.

A
So we think.

MISS LUST
That is all. Goodbye.

B
That was quick.

A
She makes a great Evangelical.

B
Unlike us.

A

Just because you can't raise the dead.

B

I'd rather join them.

A

Only a little further patience is required.

B

It seems that we have all of the hard questions and not one of the easy answers.

A

It follows that we should stick with what we know and perfect our own lives as far as we can.

B

That is an honorable occupation.

A

It might even be fun.

B

Stop! You make me giddy.

A

Radical change can do that.

B

And here comes a radical change.

A

Professor, you look beat.

PROFESSOR FISH

I thought teaching was tough. Try Royal Court Tennis with Miss Lust — or Miss Primp. It will make you wary of Feminists. They could take over the planet, the two of them.

B
I thought they had.

A
They've just kept it a secret.

PROFESSOR FISH
It's damnable.

B
Pleasure damnable?

A
At heart he's a puritan. That's what makes him such a doctrinaire left-winger.

PROFESSOR FISH
Why do I tolerate your abuse?

A
Because it's true.

B
Think about what we say. It will change you.

A
You need it.

B
You don't need degrees and books and pimply pupils, thirty year-old lecture notes and tweed jackets no one would put on a corpse. You need imagination, humor, compassion, vision, character, courage, a musical ear, a voice that charms, eyes that are open, grace of body, depth of soul, a refined intellect and a profound and real tolerance for all whom you may encounter in this life.

A
And that means that you do not take pupils - or anyone else - under your wing. You give them your wings, if that is what

they require, and wish them a fruitful journey.

> B

It is call generosity of spirit - and that is the spirit that moves the world.

> A

Look inside yourself — you will find it.

> B

And you will feel it. It is the one gift besides life - that really has value.

> PROFESSOR FISH

I feel completely inadequate.

> B

A very good place to start. Giving up the garbage is very hard, and making a present of the rest is truly frightening.

> PROFESSOR FISH

I must advance.

> A

That's it.

> B

Good luck.

> PROFESSOR FISH

It seems you will set me free.

(He goes off)

(TOFF I appears. A and B both turn their backs to him and find some activity to keep them diverted until he is almost offstage, at which time B speaks)

> B

How many friends do you have?

TOFF I
Two. And they are just like me.

B
Any enemies?

(TOFF I does not answer)

B
I don't suppose you know why?

TOFF I
Why what?

B
Why you have made yourself the Enemy of the People?

TOFF I
They are common. I am not.

B
In what way?

TOFF I
I have money, breeding and social position.

B
With two friends?

TOFF I
I could have more.

B
No doubt. I guess the money and breeding are what make you uncommon.

TOFF I
Yes. And my style.

(B winces)

B
So these are the things in life you most value.

TOFF I
Of course.

B
Do you have a heart?

TOFF I
Of course.

B
Has it been touched?
(TOFF I looks confused and a little unnerved)

B
Well?

TOFF I
I guess not.

B
Will you move over here for just a second - I want to look at your forehead.
(TOFF I moves to B. B lightly grazes TOFF's forehead with the back of his hand. TOFF does not move. Then B begins to caress the back of TOFF's head, stroking his hair. TOFF begins to cry)

B
You've never felt that before.

TOFF I
No.

B
Do you know what it is called?

TOFF I
No.

B
It is called compassion. You feel it as much as the next fellow.

Perhaps more.
(TOFF I sobs. B wraps his arms around TOFF I and holds him tightly)

   B
I double as a mother in real life, too.
(TOFF I smiles between his tears)

   B
Your tears become you much better than your airs.
(TOFF I smiles again and stops crying)

   B
Feel better?

   TOFF I
(Shyly)
Yes.

   B
Welcome to humanity. We're not such a dreadful lot, even the common ones.

   TOFF I
I expect even my type is not uncommon.

   B
You're not exactly scarce.

   TOFF I
No. Who is that?
(TOFF II enters)

   B
That's your soul-mate. He is all the things you haven't been.
(To TOFF II)
Hello!

   TOFF II
Greetings. I see we have another Toff to handle.

B
He's manageable once you touch him.

TOFF II
I'm willing.
(Embraces TOFF I)

TOFF I
Oh, I think I may melt.

B
That's one way of putting it.

A
A love-match, like ours.

TOFF II
Pardon us. We need some peace in which to breathe.

B
Of course. Love grows best in repose.

A
Shall we repose?

B
It's not yet time for us.

A
The doctor's back.

B
Fourth cousin, twelve times removed?

A
Uh-huh.

DR. GODOT
Your case has at last been correctly diagnosed.

B
Pray, tell.

DR. GODOT
Bipolar with paranoid affect.

B
Well?

DR. GODOT
At least that's what we were looking at thirty years ago.

B
Without seeing it.

DR. GODOT
Science does advance.

B
So do I.

DR. GODOT
Yes.

B
Any more up-to-the-minute bulletins?

DR. GODOT
From today's observation, I would say you are entirely cured. In fact, you are not only normal, you're unusually gifted, in mind, body and spirit. It is a pleasure, a treat, to know you.

B
I can't believe it.

A
What?

B
That he says these things.

A
They're true.

B
Why did no one ever say them before?

A
I suppose they thought you knew, and that if they told you how they saw you, they would spoil what was there.

B
And you?

A
You have always known how I felt. I was not exactly disinterested. So you discounted what I said, and rightly, I guess.

B
I'm beginning to feel human.

A
It's not so bad.

B
That's what I've always maintained.

A
Well, here we are.

DR. GODOT
That's my cue. Stay well. Flourish. You have many friends who love you, some of them even more than themselves.

A
They're only returning what they receive.

B
Goodbye.
(Tears pour down his cheeks)

A
The bearer of good news. When did the intelligentsia ever give him a fair shake?

    B
In their childhood, which they prolonged indefinitely by trying to grow up.

    A
There seems to be one person left on the dance-card: a Mr. C. Or perhaps Mr. G. I can't quite make it out.

    B
He'll pass the time.

    GODOT
Hello. I'm not late, am I?

    B
We haven't even begun waiting.

    GODOT
Any news from Mr. Godot?

    A
He hasn't arrived.

    B
There is still time.

    GODOT
Yes.

    A
We have spent the time meanwhile —

    B
Discovering ourselves.

    GODOT
That is helpful.

    A
You are Mr. G., aren't you -

B
Or Mr. C?

GODOT
Sometimes one, sometimes the other: it depends on my digestion.

B
Then you have an alias?

GODOT
Yes, for photo opportunities. I don't want to give myself away. Think what would happen to my fans.

A
Yes, baseball lives on images.

GODOT
Daniel requires attention.

B
Let me.

GODOT
Religion lives on images too, few of them accurate.

A
B and I are agnostics - we don't know.

B
And we don't want to.

A
Certainly we do. After all, what else is there to wait for besides knowledge?

GODOT
Why don't you do something?

B
Then we might find out something.

A
Horrors.

GODOT
You have started with that baby. Please continue with yourselves.

A
Double horrors.

GODOT
Not at all. It will hurt - and that is how you know you are in transit between ignorance -

A
And bliss.

GODOT
If that is what you want.

A
Are you related to Mr. Godot?

GODOT
In a way. I am his shadow.

B
Jung.

GODOT
Yes.

A
(?)
But then, where is he?

GODOT
He has come - you spoke with him.

A
We did?

B
Without knowing it.

A
Then what are you doing here?

GODOT
I'm the herald, only I come after the fact.

B
A damp squib.

GODOT
If you like.

A
Who is Jung?

B
A Swiss crackpot with too many wives.

A
Bertrand Russell had five wives, and many mistresses.

B
He needed the exercise.

A
We're of a different persuasion.

B
For these many years.

A
We have always had one another.

B
Without a ceremony, even.

A
Or the blessing of the Church.

B
Or a lawyer's fee.

GODOT
Then what binds you together is to be found within you. That is good.

A
We have had our bad times.

B
Mostly on account of very attractive adventurers: they're secretly envious of us.

A
They don't know how we do it.

GODOT
But you do it anyway: bravo!

B
Modern society seems to be based on the maxim that all rules are made to be broken.

A
And they have been -

B
And where did that leave us??

A
So here we are —

B
Making up rules —

A
For ourselves.

B
If anyone else cares to participate…
(Laughs)

A
You know, laughter is not entirely mad.

B
No, nor the wisdom of a fool.

A
It's getting late.

B
It has been for some time.

A
Perhaps he is like us.

B
Godot?

A
Yes: he only admits the mistakes he doesn't make.

B
He doesn't make mistakes, he just advertises them.

A
Why?

B
I think he needs to feel evil without being evil.

A
Are you sure he hasn't simply gone overboard?

B
Circumstances would seem to suggest it.

A
How do we rectify things?

B
Copulate.

A
Thanks.

B
I'm not kidding. It's the almost universal bid for pleasure and immortality.

A
What about the offspring?

B
They are a mirror to the character of their parents: they adopt, willy-nilly, most of their parents' faults and none of their virtues.

A
Daniel has virtues of his own.

B
And we can appreciate them only because we are not his natural parents. His natural parents would be threatened by them and throw him out.

A
They have.

B
Daniel's precocious.

GODOT
Still waiting?

A
Look at the apples!

B
We have a monopoly of the tree of knowledge!

A
I could make a pie — or applesauce, even.

GODOT
Don't eat them all at once.

A
Flowers!

B
Music!

A
Rock music!

B
Jazz!

GODOT
Gershwin!

A
I smell a roast of Virginia ham.

B
It's raining.
(A and B look at GODOT)

B
Are you Godot?

GODOT
Only you know that.

A
But it has rained.

GODOT
"The rain it raineth every day."

B
Indeed.

A
Il pleut dans mon coeur.

    B
Comme il pleut dans la ville.

    A
Good heavens, a rainbow — a triple rainbow.

    GODOT
    Thrice three makes nine,
    Swears the sage to the blind,
    The heart's ahead,
    The head's behind.

    A
Do we know you?

    GODOT
As well as yourselves.

    A
The face —

    GODOT
It is not faces that count, nor names.

    A
Are you Godot?

    GODOT
No more so than you.

    B
A real sphinx.

    GODOT
I cannot lie.

    A
What a sweet odor.

    B
Gardenias.

                GODOT
A very delicate bloom.

                A
It is beginning to make sense.

                B
How?

                A
Well, we are Godot. We have been waiting for ourselves.

                B
What next?

                A
We act.

                B
How?

                GODOT
You choose.

ACT II

    A
Well, that was tasty.

    B
Better than water and apples.

    A
Our little tree stood up remarkably well for the hanging.

    B
It's good practice. You never know who may need hanging.

    A
I'm not used to being a cannibal.

    B
Some people make it a matter of faith, though it doesn't keep the from starving.

    A
So much for Godot.
(Burps)
Very light and digestible.

    B
Yes. I expect things to improve here on out.

    A
Do you think our diet will make us divine?

    B
I don't notice any change.

    A
It reminds me of Zeus and Cronus.

    B
The same old story. If we were more numerous, we could stage Titus Andronicus. It's very true to life.

    A
Are we being wicked?

    B
Yes.

    A
Rather fun.

    B
It's a change.

    A
Do you think we'll be punished?

    B
We already have been. Now we're supplying a sufficient reason.

    A
Oh.

    B
It's a case of everything in moderation. We don't want to be too good. It would spoil the balance in our lives. And evil offers broad new opportunities for action and knowledge.

    A
I don't like it.

    B
What's wrong?

    A
It doesn't suit my idea of myself.

    B
That can be altered.

                A

I liked myself better before we ate Godot. And besides, it sets a bad example for Daniel.

                B

Oh.

                A

Daniel is the light in my life. I don't want the light to go out.
(B is silent. A starts to cry)

                B

I suppose we could hang ourselves, though it wouldn't do Daniel much good.

                A

Who will forgive us?

                B

That's the one thing we can't do for ourselves.

            GODOT

Having a picnic?
(A looks up and smiles. B appears astonished)

            GODOT

Pray, don't let me interrupt.

                A

Please do.

                B

I thought we ate you.

            GODOT

You forgot that I am Godot. And one of my ground rules is: only I can do away with myself. In any event, you both looked pretty hungry, not to say desperate.

                A

We need to be absolved.

B
(Not so contrite)
Yes.

GODOT
Granted. Anything else I can do?

A
I love you.

GODOT
(Smiles)
Thank you very much. How about Scrooge?

A
He wants to improve the world.
(General silence)

B
We hate the world at large largely because we hate ourselves.

GODOT
No joke?
(B smiles wanly. A smiles)

GODOT
I cannot be responsible for you. If you want a guide or exemplar, I am available. And there are other people available, too.

B
We don't know them.

GODOT
Yes, you do.

    A
Are they left-wing, like us?

    GODOT
Oh, the confines humans make for their minds! They are neither left nor right, nor anything in between. They are individuals, each one of them unique and self-sufficient. They take others as they come, and help them when they can. They are not afraid of their feelings. Their love lives are well-regulated: they are neither possessive nor promiscuous, nor jealous, nor cruel. Above all, they wish to give. And what they receive in return - never looked for - is my original gift to them: life.

(A and B are silent)

    GODOT
I could go on, but moralizing is only talk. What you need is a good kick in the arse.

(He chases A and B around stage. They all fall down, panting)
(MISS LUST appears)

    GODOT
Miss Lust, we need you. Desperately.

    MISS LUST
(To B)
When was the last time you tried to copulate?

    B
The Battle of Agincourt. I was violently attracted to a page-boy on the opposing side.

    GODOT
Well?

    B
Oh, we consummated our passion. He subsequently died in medias res — like a dog.

(General silence)

           GODOT
(To A)
　And you?

              A
(To B)
　I never knew about that one.
(B looks miserable)

              A
　Well, I have not fornicated since 1066. I just tease — and if things get dicey, I retreat rapidly into paranoia. In short, I am afraid.

           GODOT
　Miss Lust?

          MISS LUST
　May I quote Dido? Non ignara mali, miseris succurere disco. Or: "They called her Flower because she had been through the mill." Dear boys — you both have more company than you could imagine. That is what really keeps me busy. It is not the satisfied customer that comes back to me. It is the people with problems. And the problems are as numerous as the people. That is one reason why I like my job.

              B
　The other reason is that you like the people.

          MISS LUST
　Very good.
(B looks little less miserable)

          MISS LUST
　Now you two like men. So do I, but I am not a man. I have therefore invited a friend to join us — Mr. Tops. I am quite sure you will like each other.

(She whistles. A young man 27-30 in appearance, enters)
  Tops, these are my friends, A and B.
(They shake hands)

MISS LUST
Well, if you need help of a kind I can supply, please whistle.
(She exits)

MR. TOPS
First of all, you know that the cure for sexual problems is sex.
(A and B look a bit startled)

MR. TOPS
If you will move over here, I think I can help out. It shouldn't take long.
(They move to a remote corner of the stage)

GODOT
Busy, busy, busy.
(Lights down. Eighteen years pass. Lights up. Everyone is just as before, except the baby, who has disappeared. Enter a young man, eighteen, handsome in every way: DANIEL)

GODOT
Daniel!

DANIEL
Yes?

GODOT
We have been waiting.

DANIEL
For me?

GODOT
Who else?

DANIEL
You flatter me.

GODOT
Not at all, not at all.

DANIEL
Have you any idea where my fathers went?

GODOT
They're finishing up a seminar on sex.

DANIEL
I thought sex came naturally. Like learning how to swim.

GODOT
Some people drown.

DANIEL
Oh.

GODOT
Not you.

DANIEL
No. I like girls and they seem to like me. I have no complaints.

GODOT
Girls don't threaten you?

DANIEL
Certainly not. We understand each other.

GODOT
What about your fathers?

DANIEL
I have yet to understand them. They never talk about themselves. For all I know, they haven't had sex in 573 years. In fact, I find it difficult to think of my fathers in bed, copulating.

GODOT
They do too.

DANIEL
Oh, so that's why they're having a seminar?

GODOT
Yes. These days it's called therapy.

DANIEL
I hope it helps.

GODOT
We all do.

DANIEL
Who is that?

GODOT
Miss Primp.

MISS PRIMP
Halloo!

DANIEL
Hello.

GODOT
Hello. Back for tennis?

MISS PRIMP
I've given it up.

GODOT
Indeed.

MISS PRIMP
I now spend my time in India, helping the starving millions. But it is very difficult. The lower orders seem to like dying better than anything else. And it makes my job very hard. I am always thinking of myself as a kind of high-class undertaker. I can see that life for most of them is not worth much, but I am trying to alter that. I must help them find some good reason to live.

GODOT
It is not easy.

MISS PRIMP
No, but it is better than Royal Court Tennis. For the first time in aeons, I feel <u>useful</u>. And that makes me happy. I know the war will be long, and I shall not outlive it, but what I can do, I shall do. And that is that.

GODOT
You seem to have gained weight.

MISS PRIMP
I got married.

DANIEL
You still look fetching.

MISS PRIMP
Thank you. I suppose I can attract in a matronly way. I do not complain, neither does my husband.

DANIEL
Would you like a game of tennis?

MISS PRIMP
Thank you, but no. You are young. Try it for yourself. It may be somewhat rarefied, but that just means that you should approach it in a proper state of mind. It is not an engine for evil — certainly no more than anything else we do. Think of it as one of those deservedly obscure pleasures that pop up in most people's paths once or twice in a lifetime. Take advantage of it. That is what it is for.

DANIEL
Thank you. Thank you indeed.

GODOT
Me too.
(*MISS PRIMP exits*)

DANIEL
I hear laughter.
(GODOT smiles)
DANIEL
I think they've finished their therapy.

A
18 years!

B
Considering how long we've been here, with our problems, 18 years are not long.

A
I feel as though I've been inoculated.
(GODOT laughs)

B
Now what?

GODOT
I must move on to other puzzles. If you need help, remember: Mr. Tops is tops.

A
We will.

B
Cheerio.

DANIEL
I am reconnoitering.

A
Around us?

DANIEL
Yes, I have to. I'm eighteen and inexperienced. You two are practically Methuselahs.

        B
Charming.

        A
Shhh.

        DANIEL
My life has not been simple.
(B rolls eyes)

        B
You have much to look forward to…

        DANIEL
I'm not sure I like the example you have set.

        A
We've been in therapy for eighteen years.

        DANIEL
Precisely. You've neglected me.

        B
Good heavens.

        A
But Daniel, now we are prepared to help you.

        DANIEL
I am old enough to take care of myself.

        B
(To A)
I told you. He'll write an exposé.

        A
We'll be celebrities.

        B
(Looking at audience)
Seems we may have got there already.
(A is looking at audience, squeals in delight)

DANIEL
None of this alters the fact that I have been neglected.

B
What next?

DANIEL
I need an allowance.

B
(Laughs)
We've made one rutabaga and two carrots stretch quite far. See if you can do the same.

DANIEL
But all my friends have cars, beer, girls...

B
You earn yours.

DANIEL
I haven't ever had any of those things except girls.

B
We love you.
(This does not make much of an impression on DANIEL)

A
We are willing to help as we can, with what we know.
(DANIEL exits abruptly)

B
Anyone for tennis?

A
Do you think he'll come back?

B
Yes. With a pair of adopted parents, one of them female. We'll get over it. We have been preoccupied. I suppose we neglected him.

A
We must have: look how he turned out.

B
What I want to know is who looked after him for 18 years?

A
Miss Lust.

B
Yeoww. The high priestess of the Hedonists.

A
She always seemed nice to me.

B
Niether of us has seen her in action.

A
Well, there's nothing we can do now.

B
Our one son, gone the way of all flesh.

A
He'll recover. We did. We all grow old.

B
True.

A
Look — the skies are the color of blood.

B
We've missed dinner.

A
We talk too much.

B
No, we just concentrate on what we say.

A
And time goes by.

B
To bed! Exeunt.

(Lights up. Next morning)

GODOT
I resign.

A
Impossible.

GODOT
Nonsense. I am Godot and I resign.

B
Well? Any results?

A
Nothing noticeable.
(To GODOT)
You're still here. Intact.

GODOT
You see: No one has ever given <u>me</u> a choice.

A
You could try death again. Warmed over even.

GODOT
Once was enough.

B
Here we are, the three of us.

A
The music is nice.

B
The gardenias are definitely a plus.

GODOT
And you have each other.

B
And progeny.

A
Why not invite Miss Lust to drinks?

GODOT
I've exhausted that one.

B
Isn't lust a renewable resource?

GODOT
If you're doomed to eternity, everything becomes a renewable resource — even imagination. Sometimes I think the Universe has played a great joke on us all, including me — that it will not last forever. That it is, in fact, not indefinitely renewable.

A
You're supposed to know.

GODOT
I know.

B
It's certainly possible. Isn't there a law of thermodynamics?

GODOT
Of course! That's it. The whole machine is running down, and me with it. I knew I came to consult the right people. Brilliant.

B
Well?

A
Well what?

B
How do we spend the time that's left?

                A
You could start by blowing your nose. It's drippy.

            GODOT
It's odd.

                A
What's odd?

            GODOT
I begin to feel mortal.

                B
Welcome to the inner sanctum.

                A
Or the outer limits.

            GODOT
You're amused.

                B
Even Godot comes a cropper.

                A
But where did we all begin?

            GODOT
All out of nothing, and all back to nothing.

                A
Not even dust?

            GODOT
No. Nothing.

                A
What is nothing?

                B
That one I wouldn't touch for an eternity with Miss Lust.

> A

Or Mr. Tops.

(GODOT shrugs to say 'I don't know')

> GODOT

Nothing can be said about Nothing.

> B

If nothing can be said about it, it must be something.

> A

Touché.

> GODOT

Or nothing.

> B

Enough. Conventional conversation cannot survive on such an insubstantial plane. Let's talk about something.

(Silence)
(The TOFFS enter)

> B

Salvation.

> TOFF I

We are returning the favor.

> TOFF II

We have never been so happy.

> TOFF I

You have rescued both of us.

> TOFF II

And you have allowed us to see what we are.

> B

That you did on your own, though I thank you for the compliment.

TOFF II
We think we may adopt.

B
I can provide you with an eighteen year old.

TOFF I
We would prefer to begin with an infant.

A
That's what we did.

B
(Glumly)
Yes.

GODOT
An eighteen year old can certainly be infantile.

A
It is not easy to be a parent.

B
Yes.

TOFF II
Do you think it could be arranged?

GODOT
Without doubt. Come with me.
(GODOT, TOFF I and TOFF II exit)

B
I would have preferred a chocolate shake.

A
What?

B
When I found the money in my shoe — we might as well have spent it on ourselves.

       A
In a way, we did.

(B ?)

       A
We lived through our child.

       B
But he grew up.

       A
Precisely. And he is not now what we anticipated.

       B
I suppose he'll grow some more.

       A
If we are all lucky.

       B
And you and I may grow too.

       A
It is not impossible.

       B
In fact, he may show us something about life.

       A
It is certainly possible.

       B
Remember Mr. Tops.

       A
I do.

       B
I love you.

       A
Yes. We are a satisfactory couple.

                B
            Much more.

                A
            Yes.

                B
            Ohhhh.

                PROFESSOR FISH
            The salmon are biting. Oh, excuse me.

                B
            Not at all.

                A
            The salmon are biting?

                PROFESSOR FISH
            Yes.

                B
            In Vermont?

                PROFESSOR FISH
            Oh. They must be trout.

                B
            My favorite.

                A
            (To PROFESSOR FISH)
            He's a disciple of Julia Child.

                B
            There is nothing better for any meal or any time than a lightly poached rainbow trout freshly caught in a Vermont stream. The scenery itself is worth the trouble.

                PROFESSOR FISH
            Oh, it's no trouble, at least for me. That is why I have taken it

up. I like it.

>A

It suits you.

> PROFESSOR FISH

I know, my name.

>A

No. It is a contemplative activity and it is outdoors. It turns your attention away from yourself and fixes it on something far more grand and engrossing.

> PROFESSOR FISH

You mean Nature?

>A

Yes.

> PROFESSOR FISH

That's how I feel. I have even become acquainted with the names of trees, flowers, ferns, mosses, butterflies and birds. The outdoors has much to offer.

>B

What about your career?

> PROFESSOR FISH

I intend to make a career of Nature.

>B

Can you support yourself?

> PROFESSOR FISH

Not at first, I suppose. But with time I shall find a way. After all, this is something I truly love to do. It's the first time I have put my life on the line.

>B

Very good.

PROFESSOR FISH
I think so.

A
No more Plotinus?

PROFESSOR FISH
No.

A
Maiden-hair ferns are certainly more beautiful.

PROFESSOR FISH
I am off. Do visit if you are in the neighborhood. I shall show you my Japanese tea-garden. The water talks as it falls. And I have learned to listen.

(He goes off)

B
Well, that's a change.

(A smile)

B
Look!

A
Pozzo -

B
And Lucky.

(Enter POZZO with his rope coiled over one shoulder. LUCKY has another rope on his shoulder. They both appear in blue stripe business suits)

A
We haven't seen you in years.

POZZO
We are modifying our behaviours.

(A !)

LUCKY
I was tired of masochism.

POZZO
I was tired of my self-indulgence, amongst other things.

LUCKY
So I stood up. It hurt.

POZZO
His back was out of joint - but he stood up.

LUCKY
Yes. And then I spoke.

POZZO
I was astounded.

LUCKY
So was I.

POZZO
He said -

LUCKY
I said, "I would like something to read."

POZZO
So I gave him the Times.

LUCKY
I had no idea there were other people - other lives.

POZZO
Other than ours.

LUCKY
It floored me.
(POZZO nods his head)

LUCKY
And then I read <u>about</u> the other people. They seemed to be doing things.

POZZO
It was novel.

LUCKY
So I thought - why not me?

POZZO
But that is only half the story.

B
What's your half?

POZZO
As soon as Lucky stood up, I sat down. It was delightful. I had never thought there could be relief, but there was. And then as Lucky became human, I began to realize that I could, too. I thought, "Why not cooperate? We shall go into business for the two of us and divvy up the work and the rewards - as our talents allow." So we did.

LUCKY
We have made a success of it, too.

B
So I see.

A
Why do you keep the ropes?

POZZO
As a reminder of what in our past to avoid.

LUCKY
We have also taken up rock climbing.

                B
In Vermont?

                POZZO
How did you know?

                B
It's known for its rocks.

                A
I was born there!

                B
Yes, I know.
(To POZZO and LUCKY)
Good luck with the business.

                LUCKY
Thank you.

                POZZO
If you ever need a dollar -

                LUCKY
We are expanding. We even hire the disabled - they love to show what they can do.
(B looks at A meaningfully)

                POZZO
Good-bye.

                LUCKY
Good-bye.
(They go off)

                B
That was unexpected.

                A
No comment.

      B
I guess we're alone now.

      A
What about Godot?

      B
He's probably hanging around.

      A
But he said he had trimmed his wings.

      B
They'll grow back.

      A
And Daniel?

      B
I expect an occasional visit, wife, grandchildren.

      A
We're in our golden years now.

      B
They're an improvement - thanks to everyone -

      A
And us!

      B
Well, we did put some effort into changing. But I still have no desire to do a lot of radical nonsense. Just living is radical enough.

      A
Where does the time go?

      B
I thought we had figured that one out - from Nothing to Nothing.

A
There is very much in between.

B
Yes, as much as anyone, including Godot, could want. Quote the Bard -

A
Ripeness is all.

B
We are ripe. We may be a little rotten.

A
It is very quiet.

B
Our tree is asleep.

A
After all those apples.

B
I have the trots.
(Leaves the stage running)

A
Au revoir.
(A putters around till B returns)

B
That was close.

A
Have some cheese.
(They smile)

B
I used to play the piano.

A
Badly.

B
It drove everyone up the wall.

A
It was kind of you to let them down.

B
It's my specialty. Up and down.

A
Do you realize that we're very near our two thousandth anniversary?

B
So soon?

A
What we have seen!

B
Beats this place.

A
Nonsense. It's time we rested. We can savor our memories.

B
Why ask for trouble?

A
I thought we had reformed you.

B
You did. I just bounced back. Everything has its natural shape - and I have mine. Please respect it. If it comes to trouble, that is my concern.

A
You are very prickly this evening.

B
I want you.

A
Well, that was easy. Now?

B
Yes, while there's still some light. I hate dining in the dark.

A
Ooohh!
(B growls. Lights fade. Night)
(Another morning)

A
Do you like the gardenias?

B
At a distance.

A
What?

B
They're very sweet, and sweet things invariably end up costing you something.

A
Like a rotten tooth.

B
Or a broken heart.

A
I feel ambitious.

B
Maybe today you'll do something.

A
I always used to think ambition unseemly - from a radical point of view.

B
How absurd. The radical are more overblown than everyone else combined. That is why they are radical.

A
Then ambition is all right?

B
It depends whether you want to live on rutabagas and carrots.

A
I could use an Egg McMuffin occasionally.

B
And I am still on the track of a chocolate shake.

A
Perhaps you could form a business.

B
A going concern?

A
Yes! Yes! We could market our concern. Mr. Tops showed us all his tricks. They are not patented. And Miss lUst said there's plenty of demand. And we have apples to eat till we accumulate some capital. In fact, our apples are our capital.

B
Metaphorically speaking.

A
Yes. Oooh - I'm feeling more ambitious than ever.

B
Don't you need a degree to do this sort of thing?

A
(Deflated but not defeated)
I shall get one. Perhaps Professor Fish could help.

B
I think it would be more realistic to go into apples. We have enough. Besides, at our age we're supposed to decline gracefully into the grave.

A
Well I won't. I wish to be of use till the end.

B
Here's Daniel. If it's money you want, look in your shoe.

DANIEL
(Mystified)
I came to say good-bye.

B
How considerate.

A
Oh, Daniel, we apologize if we have made mistakes.

B
We hope you do not compound them.
(DANIEL looks startled)

A
We wanted to give you a happy past.
(DANIEL appears sad, along with A and B, especially A)

A
We did not intend to fail. It just feel out that way. We would like to make peace. We would even offer you what's left of our lives to help you through all that lies hidden ahead of you. We love you.

B
Indeed we do.
(DANIEL is totally disarmed)

      A
We all know what we have seen. The problem is how to turn it to account.

      B
If you leave, go quietly...
(Silence)

    DANIEL
I'm thinking.

      B
(To A)
For God's sake, don't tell him to <u>do</u> something.

    DANIEL
Do we have to stay near the Outer Hebrides?

      A
I've always adored London.

      B
Or Paris.

    DANIEL
We'll be destitute to start.

      B
I think we can manage that one.

      A
We always have.

    DANIEL
Agreed.

      A
Agreed.

      B
Agreed.
(Music: Spring, from Vivaldi's <u>Four Seasons</u>)

GODOT
(Enters)
I hear you three are off to London.

B
How did you know?

GODOT
I am all ears. May I come too? With you?

A
Of course.

B
As long as you don't pull rank.

GODOT
I wouldn't dare.

A
Of course not.

DANIEL
Otherwise you would give yourself away.
(B smiles)

DANIEL
Be subtle.

GODOT
I shall be invisible. Metaphorically speaking.

B
Do we have a plan of action?
(Enter POZZO and LUCKY)

A
We are blessed.
(To POZZO and LUCKY)
You said your enterprise was expanding. Could we fill in the empty spaces?

POZZO
Of course, eh, Lucky?

LUCKY
No problem.
(To GODOT)
You too?

GODOT
Why not?

LUCKY
No joke?

GODOT
Of course not. Even I need an occupation of some kind. And what you offer is highly novel for me. I look forward to working with you.

A
Me, too.

DANIEL
Let's make it unanimous.
(They do)

A
Look, our tree! It's wilting.

B
It weeps for thee.

A
Where shall we ever find another?

B
All we need to do is plant a seed.

A
Which you have!

   B
In abundance.
   DANIEL
Off!
(They all leave. TOFF II appears and reads)
   TOFF II
Keep to poverty, and a poet's candid soul, the love you give your friend, I'll give my foe and not be poor thereby.
(TOFF I enters and reads)
   TOFF I
…Who loves most loves secretly…

-*FINIS*-